I HAVE A DEGREE IN ACTING ...
NOW WHAT?

by

Meghan Deanna Smith

ISBN: 978-1-7342058-0-0 (Print)
ISBN: 978-1-7342058-1-7 (Digital)

Library of Congress Control Number: 2019917236

Editor: Jennifer Pecoraro & Curtis Kingsley
Cover Design: Cassandra Santa Maria
Photos: Tony David Photography (pg. 6) & Elizabeth
Snyder Photography (pg. 88 & Back Cover)

Printed in the United States of America
First Edition

Meghan Deanna Smith
Los Angeles, CA

@megdeannasmith

ACKNOWLEDGMENTS

Curtis: the only reason this book came to fruition is because of your never-ending love, help, and editing assistance. You're so incredible. Thank you, BB.

Mom & Dad: thank you for the endless support and for always encouraging my weirdness.

To All My Rescue Dogs (Past, Present, & Future): You haven't technically helped me write this book, nor can you read ... but you have filled my life with joy, and I am grateful for the pawprints you've left on my heart. Please adopt, don't shop.

TABLE of CONTENTS

INTRODUCTION

Hello beautiful reader. First and foremost, I think you're a pretty fantastic human being for not only buying/borrowing/e-reading my glorious book, but also for taking a major step toward bettering your career. Secondly, I know what you're thinking: Oh my gosh, that adorably attractive girl on the cover is the author of this book? How have I never heard of her? Why isn't she a famous millionaire? Shouldn't the two of us be sipping margaritas together in Belize?

Now yes, it is hard to believe that I, Meghan Deanna Smith, am not a famous millionaire (YET). But what I am is a working actress who's pretty qualified to help guide you, my remarkable reader, through the crazy journey that lies ahead once you have that problematic Acting Degree. Oh, and maybe one day we will enjoy fruity cocktails together in a tropical setting. Who knows, the possibilities are endless. But I digress. Let's get back to this book and how it will help advance your professional goals.

A few years ago, I graduated with a Bachelor of Fine Arts in Theater Performance from a private college in New York state. In other words, I'm $37,000 in debt. Upon graduating, I realized I had read dozens of performance books, taken countless workshops, and was familiar with pretty much every acting technique there is from Stanislavsky to Keanu Reeves. Basically, I knew how to act the crap out of any material, and I was given all the tools needed to analyze any script. But what I quickly realized was that I had no clue how to actually GET the role. I knew exactly what to do once I was cast, but getting cast immediately seemed impossible.

I borrowed tons of acting books from the library, praying they'd reveal some big secret my professors seemed to have hidden from me. But it was always the same. The books taught me how to act—not how to get cast, or how to get an agent, or most importantly, how to be able to financially live off acting. Thus, I had to learn the hard way, through experience. I moved to a town just outside of New York City for a bit and then made the big trek to Los Angeles where I basically learned how to survive as a starving artist (emphasis on starving). I figured out which acting websites posted castings, I discovered how to get an agent, and I learned the importance of marketing myself. But all of this took time. It didn't happen overnight and unfortunately my daily mantra turned into: Gosh, I wish they taught me this in college.

Throughout my journey after graduation, I kept making mental notes about my experiences. I often thought, "Oooo when I'm famous and people will pay to just be in my presence, I should tell young aspiring actors this helpful tip... Or that... Or this!" And then I realized I did not have to wait until I was a household name. In fact, even though I'm not filthy stinking rich off of acting, I am still a working actor, I'm still living in the entertainment capital of the world, and I already have so much information to share. That's how this book endeavor began. I don't want anyone pursuing a career in acting to feel confused or alone or as if their degree was pointless. Although the majority of my advice will be targeted toward the film industry (because that's what currently pays my bills), a lot of my advice is also applicable to the theater world. After all, my degree is in Theater Performance, and the two industries aren't that different from one another.

So, long story short, this book is designed to guide you, help you, and make you feel like you can totally survive in the ginormously scary acting industry. Enjoy.

P.S. This book is a bunch of advice—not promises or concrete facts. If you follow my suggestions and don't become successful, please don't sue me! I'm just kidding... but really, don't sue me...

CHAPTER ONE

HEADSHOTS, REELS, AND WEBSITES (Oh My!)

So by now, you've at least heard of headshots, reels, and websites. However, after graduating college, I only had one of the three—headshots—which was no bueno. To be honest, my headshots weren't even that good. In my opinion, having these three things is ESSENTIAL to booking work and being taken seriously. I'm going to break them all down individually.

HEADSHOTS

First and foremost, let's talk about the all-important shots of your head. A headshot is an eight-inch by ten-inch color photo of your beautiful face. You read that correctly: eight inches by ten inches, not the standard printer paper size of eight and a half by eleven inches. This is supposedly because in the early acting days, photos could only be printed on legitimate photo paper sizes. Anything smaller than an eight by ten would be too tiny to discern, and anything larger would be superfluous. I can only assume the real reason is because the acting gods want to make life more difficult for us. Anyways, I'm also sure someone's already told you how crucial a good photo is to getting you in the casting room. But let me reiterate it. GOOD HEADSHOTS ARE CRUCIAL IN GETTING YOU INTO THE CASTING ROOM!

Often times, Casting Directors (CDs) are looking through dozens upon dozens of photos. They're not intently examining your long list of skills, they're not looking at what acting workshops you attended, and they're not calling your Great Aunt Milly to hear how proud she is of you for pursuing your dreams. Instead, they're perusing through online pictures the size of your thumb, trying to find faces that stand out.

There are a few tips I've learned over the years:

1. Do not do anything to distract the CD from your face and eyes. That includes tilting your head, putting your hand on your face, or wearing distracting jewelry. You need to be looking directly into the camera and the framing should be straight on. For a solid year, I

thought this was an excellent headshot. Spoiler Alert: It wasn't. Now don't get me wrong, it is a beautiful photo. But, as seductively charming as I look, many agents and CDs kept telling me how distracting they found the hand near my face. Apparently, caressing your neck with your fingers is very High School Senior Portrait-esque, so just don't do it. Additionally, you can see that my face is not straight on, it's artistically tilted. This too is a no-no. Your eyes should be on the same plane. A little tilt is fine, but a good rule of thumb is if you can notice the tilt immediately, it's too distracting.

2. Be open to trying different "character looks," as this is a growing trend in the headshot game. When an agent first told me I needed seven new headshots with seven different "looks," I laughed out loud. No, really, I chuckled in his face and was then scolded for not taking him seriously. Apparently if a CD is trying to book you for a guest spot on a network drama as a nurse, they want to see a picture of you as a nurse. Why? Because CDs are lazy and do not want to have

to do the extra work of picturing you as a nurse, they want to see you in actual scrubs. (If you're a Casting Director and you're reading this, you are NOT lazy! In fact, you're perfect and amazing and should cast me immediately.)

So, as crazy as it sounds, you're going to need numerous headshots with numerous looks. That means goth, hippie, computer hacker, cowboy, hooker, cop, pregnant zombie who's addicted to avocados, etc. Okay, so maybe not the zombie one, just making sure you're still paying attention. But as laughable as all those looks sound, they will get you booked. I am capable of playing a pretty large age range, so I also needed headshots that made me look young enough to attend high school and other headshots showing I'm old enough to be drinking in a bar.

You might have been told to, "know your brand," and stick with your specific "look." And yes, knowing your brand/look/strengths is imperative. If you cannot believably play a high schooler, then certainly don't take a picture portraying yourself as one. Similarly, if your acting style is darker and sarcastic, taking pictures with a cheesy grin while wearing a cheerleader outfit is probably pointless. However, when you're first starting off and self-submitting for things without any representation, you're going to want to apply for as many different jobs as possible.

This is because, obviously, the more things you submit for, the higher the chance you'll be brought in for an audition. Hence, having a young dad picture for example, in addition to a sultry, soap opera-type shot can be super useful! Capturing diverse looks will expand your chances of getting work.

3. There is a difference between a commercial headshot and a theatrical headshot. A commercial headshot is typically for, you guessed it, commercials! Theatrical headshots are used for film and television. The differences between the two aren't too drastic, but they are significant.

    A commercial headshot should be your most inviting look. You should be smiling and showing your teeth. When you don't show your teeth in a commercial headshot, the CD automatically assumes you have unattractive teeth. So, show off those pearly whites Mom and Dad paid thousands of dollars for! Unless you really don't have the greatest teeth, in which case you should master the toothless smile. For the most part, your commercial headshot should be warm, wholesome, and a little generic. Think of the kind of people you normally see in commercials. They're usually your average happy American.

    Lately, there has been a new tendency of commercials featuring actors that look more like real people do. This means, we're seeing less and less glamourous people featured in commercial content, and instead more plain or quirky looks. So, opting to have a commercial headshot with your glasses on, or maybe one with your bushy mustache, can be a very useful thing to have in your back pocket.

Theatrical headshots can be much more serious. You do not need to smile if you don't want to and if you're a dramatic actor, showing a deeper, more dramatic side can work for this. Since these are the pictures you'll be submitting for scripted, fictional content, you will want a look that works for both hour-long dramas in addition to thirty-minute sitcoms. However, unless they're your "character looks," you do not need to go overboard with your commercial and theatrical options.

Ladies, you should also avoid wearing tons of make-up or curling/straightening your hair if it is not something you would normally do before an audition. When you walk into the casting room, the CD will expect the person standing before them to actually look like the person in the headshot. CDs definitely feel deceived if the actor doesn't resemble the picture sent in. You want the CD focusing on your performance and personality, not the fact that you look nothing like your headshot. It's vital to remember that your headshot does not need to be a picture in which you look your absolute best. I kept getting hung up on wanting to look "pretty" in my headshots instead of "book-able." Looking kind of dumb or not overly glamorous can actually be a good thing because not every role requires a glamorous look.

Also, I was once told, "Your headshot doesn't stand out. You just look like a white girl smiling in a pink shirt." I had trouble understanding the issue because I *am* a white girl and I *was* wearing a pink shirt. Figuring out how to make your picture "stand out" while also "looking like the real you" is hard. You can't change your face, but something you can adjust is the background color. About ten years ago, outdoor headshots were all the rage. And although natural lighting is still an incredible asset for photos, having a simple, solid colored, bright background is way more beneficial than an artsy outdoor brick wall. Remember to keep in mind how small the thumbnail of your headshot will be online and consider choosing a bright blue or pale pink background for example. It might seem a little gaudy, but that pop of color could make the difference between a CD clicking on your photo versus someone else's. Keep in mind, you still need to be the star of the photo, not your background.

4. Be prepared to spend money on new headshots. Whatever agency you sign with will tell you that you need new headshots. It does not matter if you JUST got them done a week prior to signing with them, I

guarantee they will say, "You need better photos." Then they will proceed to give you a list of their favorite photographers, and I promise it will cost you hundreds of dollars.

That being said, I've been known to weasel my way out of getting new pictures by using my awesome charm and evasiveness, but I don't recommend it. What I do recommend is spending a little money at first (or recruiting a talented photographer friend) to take some decent pictures. Use those decent photos to submit to agencies and save some money in the meantime. Then when an agent wants you and inevitably demands you get new headshots, you'll have put aside some money for it. I know, I know, I'm a genius. You must learn to invest in your career.

Side Note: If an agent *demands* you must have photos taken by a specific photographer, it's most likely a scam. In these scenarios both the agent and photographer will have struck up a deal with one another, and both profit off of the actor. There is no need for you to have photos taken by anyone you don't feel comfortable paying.

5. Don't be afraid to be vocal in a professional photo-shoot. I've never met an actor who loves their headshot, but why? You're there in the room, you're paying the photographer for his or her time and talent, and you now know what industry professionals are

looking for in a headshot. You should have a say, so speak up.

As uncomfortable as you might feel, you need to ask to see the photos as they are being taken and make adjustments accordingly. Also, if a photographer tries to make you do some bizarro stuff that you know you're not going to use, respectfully object. Don't waste your time or money by allowing the photographer to do what they want and not what you want. You're the one who's going to be looking at this photo every day, not them. They're technically your employee, so be bossy!

6. Avoid getting your headshots printed from a headshot printing website or shop. Many professors or agents will recommend you get your photos printed from these types of places because they'll be the accurate eight-inch by ten-inch size, they'll be on nice photo paper, and you get a pretty good discount if you buy in bulk. Here's why this is a bad idea in my opinion: Firstly, physical headshots are becoming obsolete! Most everything is done on the internet nowadays and you're rarely required to bring a paper copy with you to an audition. Yes, you will go on the occasional audition or cattle call that will require a printed-out headshot, but now that we're in the 2020's things just aren't done that way anymore. Most everything is electronic.

This is why I feel headshot printer shops are a bad idea. The only way you get good prices from these places is by purchasing an enormous number of headshots at a time. As amazing as it would be to go on 100 auditions a year, it's just not realistic. Plus, it's even more unrealistic to think that each one of those 100 auditions will ask for paper copies of your stuff.

Also, yes, it's nice that the photos come the proper size, but here's another secret: scissors can cut paper to any size you want! Crazy, right?! Instead, I suggest going to any print shop or office supply store to get your headshots printed out on photo paper. You can print out as many or as few as you like. This way you can get, for example, only three goth headshots because those auditions will be less common. It is much more economical to go to an office supply store once a month to print out pictures as you run out, rather than to waste a ton of money on a hundred headshots that will just collect dust.

I usually make an eight-inch by ten-inch box on a Word document. I add my headshot to the center of the box and put my stage name at the bottom of the box. You should always include your name in addition to the photo. I save it as a PDF, put it on a thumb drive, and carry it with me everywhere. Then when I need it, I stop at Staples, print the PDF, cut around the eight by ten box and voilà! A perfect, cheap headshot!

It can also be advantageous to use both methods. So, for example, you can use a headshot print shop to print 100 copies of your most generic, bookable look knowing they'll be the perfect size/quality. Then, you can use an office supply store to print out a few each of all your character looks. Ultimately, you'll learn which photos you use the most once you start auditioning and then you can decide which shots to invest money on printing out.

P.S. A stage name is essentially another term for your professional name. People will also refer to it as your "SAG Name." Once you start getting roles, you want to make sure that you're being credited as your stage name. For many people, their stage name is the same as their birth name. However, when determining if you want to keep your birth name as your professional title, a good idea is to check the list of SAG actors to see if someone is already registered with your name. Two people cannot register with the same name, so if you join the union second, you'll have to choose something else.

For example, my SAG name is Meghan Deanna Smith. I use my middle name for two reasons. The first being because my parents named me after a *Star Trek: The Next Generation* character and I want my family's trekkie legacy to live long and prosper. Secondly, because the name "Meghan Smith" alone is pretty common. I recommend picking a stage name ASAP! The sooner you've established your professional title, the sooner all your credits will match. You don't want a CD to get to know you as one name and then not recognize your name when you change it two years later.

REELS

Besides an amaze-balls headshot, the second most important thing to have as an actor is a reel. When I first tried getting professional representation, I had no idea what a reel really was. I remember an agent emailing me saying that before they'd agree to meet with me, they'd need to watch my reel. That was the first time I remember thinking college screwed me. Okay, maybe not screwed me, but definitely didn't prepare me fully. (Full Disclosure: I loved my university, am incredibly grateful for everything it taught me, and I miss it very much. Go Purple Eagles!)

Okay so anyway, I scrambled to email anyone I'd ever done a project for (stage and film) and begged them for the footage. A reel is essentially a video compilation of work you've done to demonstrate your ability. It's typically under five minutes, although many agents and CDs want it much, *much* shorter. I'd aim for under two minutes. A CD watching your reel is going to get a feel for you after the first 30 seconds and will most likely exit out shortly after. Thus, put your best clip first! Also, it is

VERY IMPORTANT to start with a close-up of your face, showing you speaking. Do not start your reel with someone else's face or someone else's line. The CD is going to watch your video to learn what *you* sound and look like, not someone else!

Also, I recommend splitting up your footage into two categories: comedy and drama. Mixing dramatic clips with comedic clips is discombobulating. If you're watching an actor bawling his eyes out and then the next second he's cracking jokes, you're less likely to believe him. If you're submitting for a dramatic role, the CD does not need to know you can be funny. And vice versa, if the role is comedic, you do not need to prove that you can shed a realistic tear. Brand and market yourself even within your reels.

There are five other main reels in the industry: a commercial reel, a stand-up reel, a hosting reel, a voice-over reel and a theater reel.

A commercial reel is a compilation of any commercials you have acted in. You can use clips from television commercials in addition to any online advertisements you've acted in.

A stand-up reel is pretty self-explanatory. If you're a comedian who does stand-up, you should have a friend film some of your open mic nights. Then, pick your best jokes that got the most laughs and sew them all together into a short video.

A hosting reel is trickier. You can't just ask your friend to film you "hosting." Typically, a hosting reel is a compilation of clips that show off your ability to read from a teleprompter, interview people on the street, or introduce celebrities. If you did any anchoring for your college's Communications department, I recommend starting with those clips. Then, as you get more hosting work, piece those gigs together for your hosting reel. If you've got a good enough camera, microphone, and some actor friends, you could potentially fake a "man-on-the-street" interview, but make sure it doesn't look like you're talking to your next-door neighbor on your Dad's old camcorder.

Voice-over reels consist of a minute or two of your voice-over work/abilities. Even if you've never booked a professional voice-over job before, most smart phones have decent enough microphones that you can record something right from home. The voice-over CDs will be able to tell it's a homemade reel, but it will certainly be better than nothing. You can search voice-over reels online to get an idea of the kind of content you should replicate. The voice-over industry is a great way for struggling artists to make a pretty penny while also still acting, so don't rule this out as a potential career path!

A theater reel is also pretty self-explanatory. Take clips of your various live theater performances (preferably from well-known shows) and make a short video displaying your talent. You can use community theater footage, college footage, or competition footage. If you're still in college, I recommend taking advantage of your school's stage. Use it to perform a scene that you and a peer have been working on and film it. Just set up the tripod to cut out the lack of audience and you've immediately got excellent footage for a theater reel! In fact, do this with as many different scenes and scene partners, and you'll have an excellent variety of footage (just make sure you're not wearing the same outfit in all of the clips).

You will be posting all of these reels to casting websites. It is a huge advantage for you to have reels up on these websites because your submissions will appear higher on their submission feed than those without. There are also a few other videos you're going to want to have up on these sites. They're not necessarily "reels." They're more clips of your skills.

For example, many roles require singing ability. Therefore, find or create a video of you singing a song (preferably one you're decent at!). Boom. Instant proof you can sing. Another requirement you'll sometimes see is model experience. If you can put together some footage of you on a modeling shoot, this will be a huge advantage over others. This is also something you can try to fake if need be: ask a friend to be the "photographer" and another friend to take video footage of the photo shoot. Piece that together into a twenty second clip and you've got yourself a modeling video! Other skills you should have clips of are things like: athletic abilities, dance skills, quirky talents, etc. Casting notices will say things such as, "Looking for REAL soccer players." You'll be able to confidently submit for the part if you've got actual footage of you playing soccer. Plus, the CD will be able to *see* that you can actually play and won't be worried about whether or not you've lied.

WEBSITES

People are going to want proof that you're talented, professional, and capable. Unfortunately, they're not just going to take your word for it. Trust me, I've tried. That's where the importance of a website (or at least an online presence) comes into play. This way, no matter who you're communicating with, be it an agent, a director, or really anyone in the industry, you'll have something concrete to prove your capabilities.

Often times people will say, "send me your stuff." Instead of having to send them numerous pictures, PDFs, video clips, and hyperlinks, risking that they may not look at it all, you can give them everything in one place by creating a website for yourself. If you don't want to splurge on purchasing your own domain (because let's face it, if you're reading this book you're probably a poor artist), there are several free website generators that will do the trick. I personally liked using www.wix.com for my first free website. Upload all your different headshots, your resumé, your reels, and any other links.

Social media is huge, so including links to your Facebook, Twitter, and Instagram make sense, in addition to a link to your IMDb (Internet Movie Database) page. Oh yeah, let's talk about IMDb.

As soon as you can, you'll want to upload at least one picture to IMDb and start seeking gigs that will guarantee an IMDb credit. Even indie films have IMDb pages nowadays, so you don't have to wait until you're cast in a Spielberg film to get credit online. Creating an IMDb profile costs money, but it's worth it. The sooner you have an IMDb page with an actual picture instead of the default creepy, gray shadow person thumbnail, the sooner you'll be taken seriously.

You'll hear a lot that you're a product and you need to sell your brand. That's what these three things will ensure. Headshots, reels, and websites prove that you're taking your career seriously and you know what you're doing. It's kind of like that phrase, "Dress for the job you want, not the job you have." In this case, market yourself as if you've been successfully working for ten years and people will pay attention.

CHAPTER TWO

TRAINING AND COMPETITIONS

I'm going to share with you a few things that have helped me to market myself.

TRAINING

If you're reading this book, you most likely have a degree BECAUSE THE BOOK IS TITLED I HAVE A DEGREE. Which is awesome because you've already got something to list under the training section of your resumé. However, if you don't have a degree, that's awesome too because that means you haven't sold your soul to Sallie Mae and won't be in astronomical debt for the rest of your life! If you do have a degree, here's a piece of advice: don't list the year you graduated on your resumé or website. If you put a year down, a Casting Director (CD) can assume how old you are, and you don't want that to affect how old you can play. For example, I have a baby face and have consistently been booked as an "18TLY" or "18TPY." They stand for "18 to look younger" and "18 to play younger." In other words, I'm a legal adult, yet I can play ages younger than 18. No joke, I was once cast as a middle schooler when I was in fact old enough to drink. So basically, don't include anything on your resumé that's going to imply age. A CD could think you look 30, but when they find out you're actually 20, they may look at you differently and cast someone who's actually the age of the character. Therefore, ambiguity is key.

Also, if you have a degree, you've probably attended a couple of workshops throughout your educational journey. These free workshops with guest speakers are instant resumé boosters and would typically cost hundreds of dollars to attend in either Los Angeles or New York City. Including workshops under your training section helps demonstrate you have obtained knowledge from an industry professional. Some Commercial Agents won't even sign you unless you have a least one commercial workshop under your belt. So, if you didn't attend any workshops while you were in school, or if you didn't go to school, I recommend taking a couple workshops not only for the marketing boost, but also because you'll learn some valuable tips. At the end of the day, knowledge is power. If you haven't studied at a University, I also recommend taking a few acting classes in your local entertainment industry hub. Again, it not only helps market you as a trained performer, but it will also make you a better actor. Win, win.

As far as Casting Director workshops go, they're helpful for a few things, but they will NOT get you cast in an upcoming television series. That's just not how it works. Many actors think if they take a workshop with the CD of *Stranger Things*, next week they'll have a regular part on the series. Uh, nope. Here's your reality check: CD workshops help expand the training section on your resumé, teach you a few industry tricks, and potentially allow you to build a relationship with a working industry professional. In a perfect world, you develop a mini relationship with the CD hosting the workshop and are able to use their name as a reference for agencies. CD referrals are number one for getting your foot into the door at an agency. However, just because you do a CD workshop does not guarantee you'll be able to use their name as a reference, and it's possible you won't have made a connection with them. Hope for the best, but go into the workshop with realistic expectations and understand that nothing else may come from it.

Speaking of Casting Directors, I'm going to tell you a sad story about myself. One day, I walked into the Samuel French Bookshop on Sunset Boulevard in Hollywood and purchased a directory that included dozens of CDs, what shows they cast for, and their office address. I then printed out SIXTY headshots, SIXTY resumés, purchased SIXTY envelopes, personally wrote SIXTY individual cover letters, and paid for them to be shipped. I spent over $150, but was confident something was to come of it. Guess what? NOTHING CAME FROM IT. I didn't receive a single response. Ever. I was devastated, both emotionally and financially. It really drove home the point that if the CD isn't reaching out to you, or if you don't have a personal connection to them, mailing out your goods accomplishes nothing. Someone in Los Angeles taught me that this industry isn't about "who you know," but instead it's all about "who knows you." For example, you may meet the executive producer of a popular soap opera at a networking party, but if they don't think of you and reach out to you, the connection is pointless. So, make friendships and be memorable. Stand out so that the important people will think of you and will reach out.

My final piece of training advice, whether you're a comedic or dramatic actor, is to take an improv class. Now, if you're the next Meryl Streep and you just scoffed at that last sentence because you're an incredibly talented dramatic actor who doesn't need to learn how to tell a joke, then shame on you for doubting me! Just hear me out. When I say take an improv class, I do not mean an extra-curricular class offered at your University, or signing up for a Saturday morning community theater improv class. I mean you should pay to attend one of the top-notch, professional improv institutes: The Second

City, Upright Citizens Brigade (UCB), Groundlings, or Improv Olympic (iO). For a comedic actor who wants to be taken seriously, you MUST have at least one of these on your resumé. You can't just be funny, you need to prove you've been professionally taught how to be funny. Once you tell someone you do comedy and that you studied at Second City—uh you know, the place where Tina Fey, Steve Carell and Bill Murray all came from— they will immediately take you ten times more seriously.

Improv is not just pretending to be a grandma with a British accent on planet Mars. It's about mastering the technique of "yes, and..." way more than creating quirky characters or telling funny jokes. That's where it comes into play for all types of actors trying to get representation or book gigs. I had no idea that Commercial CDs or agencies search for improv training, but they do. A lot of projects do not have concrete scripts and they want to rely on the actors to create worthy content. Agents will tell you to take an improv class because they know the CDs are looking for that skill. I had taken improv classes from Buffalo ComedySportz, a great improv establishment, but I wasn't taken seriously until I also had Second City Chicago on my resumé. (Second City is not paying me to advertise for them, although they should. In fact, if you're Second City's PR person, just find me on social media, private message me, and I'll tell you where to send the check.)

One final piece of advice as far as the improv stuff goes. I'm not, by any means, saying devote all your time and money to an improv school. Many of the schools are conservatory-esque and have numerous class levels before you can "graduate." THIS IS UNNECESSARY. Seriously, all you have to do is attend a 101- level class and you can simply put on your resumé:

"Upright Citizens Brigade, Teacher Name"

Many of these schools even offer week-long intensives so you can get it done and over within just a week. That's how I was able to study both improv and sketch writing when I was at Second City. Intensives saved my life! (Side Bar: Thanks again Auntie Norma and Uncle Allen for letting me stay at your house while I studied at Second City!) I also attended an open house at The Groundlings in Los Angeles. One Saturday they offered three one-hour courses for five dollars each to give you a taste of their program. I did all three courses for only fifteen dollars total and was subsequently able to get some Groundlings experience without paying an arm and a leg.

So anyway, the sooner you can get some legit improv training on your resumé, the sooner you'll become desirable.

COMPETITIONS

Competitions can be more beneficial than you think. The first competition I want to discuss is called IMTA (International Modeling and Talent Association). It's a week-long convention that consists of modeling and acting competitions that dozens of agents/managers attend. It's well known in the sense that it launched the careers of huge stars such as Ashton Kutcher, Eva Longoria, Katie Holmes, and Jessica Biel. It costs money, but I decided during college that I was going to save up in order to compete in it after I graduated. I went into the competition thinking no matter what, this is an amazing opportunity to be seen by agents, something that can be almost impossible with no connections. So, I competed, and much to my surprise, I was called back by a dozen agencies and named IMTA's Actor of the Year. I pooped my pants (because of shock and excitement--I don't have an actual pooping problem).

Now, I'm not telling you this to brag about my ability, nor is IMTA paying me to mention them. I'm telling you this because it immediately became an amazing way to market myself. From that moment on, I was able to describe myself as an award-winning actress, following in the footsteps of some of the best of the best. It gave me confidence and it was a remarkable marketing tool. Up until that point, I had nothing to prove I was talented. So, although I'm not telling you to compete in IMTA specifically, I am suggesting you look into prestigious competitions, work your butt off, and use those as a way to market yourself. Even if you don't place in a category or don't win an overall title, it's still an amazing way to be seen by industry professionals for whom you wouldn't normally be able to perform. Think of them as Actor Showcases. I remember one girl competed and didn't win any categories, but her look was so quirky/unique that tons of agencies called her back. What I'm saying is that giving yourself an opportunity to win an award and perform in front of industry professionals can only help, not hurt.

I mentioned that IMTA gave me confidence, but I want to reiterate how powerful confidence truly is. In fact, being confident changed my career significantly and to this day is one of my biggest keys to success. Once I truly believed in myself and my talent, I stopped trying so hard to prove it to others. I was much more relaxed and more capable of showing my true self in audition rooms.

Also, you don't need an award to prove to yourself that you're talented. Look inward, work hard, and believe. The saying is true: "If you don't believe in yourself, why should others?" Plus, having confidence in audition settings calms your nerves dramatically. Instead of worrying if you're good enough or if they'll like your style, you'll go into the room knowing you're good enough. Confidence instantly makes you able to focus on your script and your character, ensuring a great audition.

If you don't get booked at that point, you know it had nothing to do with your preparation or read, you just simply didn't fit the character.

CHAPTER THREE

Oh, resumé, you dirty minx. You are both incredibly important and utterly useless. Ok, maybe "utterly useless" is a little hyperbolic. But, there have been many times I've felt my resumé didn't matter.

A resumé is an eight-inch by ten-inch piece of paper that you staple to the back of your headshot. Why is your resumé also only eight by ten instead of the standard paper size of eight and a half by eleven? Because the entertainment industry is a cruel, dark world. I still don't understand why the industry hasn't grown to accept standard size paper over the years, but I do know that it's a real pain in the butt having to cut an inch and a half off every single headshot and resumé. Nevertheless, anything for the craft, right? The reason you're told to staple your resumé to the back (as opposed to double sided printing) is because the idea is that you're constantly getting new credits to add to your resumé, so you'll constantly be removing your old resumé and stapling your new one. You may get a new role once a month (I WISH), but only change your headshots once a year. It's an industry standard.

Obviously, having legitimate credits to beef up your resumé is key, but what I've discovered is that it is impossible to predict what is going to be important to each individual Casting Director (CD). Not everyone enjoys the same food, and not every CD cares about the same things. Some will love that you have a college degree, some will hate it. Some will adore that you trained at Stella Adler Studio, and some won't have a clue what that is. What you want to do is focus on the gigs you've done that have name recognition. For example, if you get cast as a supporting role in a non-union Lifetime movie with a forgettable title, directed by a nobody director, the important thing to include on your resumé is Lifetime. A CD won't care about the director if it's someone they've never heard of, but they will care about Lifetime because it's a network they recognize.

The same thing is true with your training section. You may be so proud of your Acting Degree from your hometown's community college, but unless your professors are nationally known, there is no point in including that Professor Joe Shmoe taught you ballet. Instead, the important things to include would be that you have a degree and ballet experience. "Keep it simple, stupid" is a good thing to remember when constructing your resumé.

At the top of your resumé is where you include your name, contact information, physical stats, and your union status. (If you're not in the union, don't put "non-union," just leave it blank. If you are in the union or about to be, put either "SAG," "SAG-AFTRA," or "SAG-e," which means SAG Eligible). Once you get representation, you'll swap out your contact information for your agent's. I also like to include an additional small headshot (a different photo than the one on front) in one of the corners. I do this so when someone is looking at my resumé, not my headshot, my face is still present. It psychologically helps them remember you better and it gives you a chance to show a slightly different look. For example, if you wear glasses, your eight by ten headshot can show off your beautiful frames, but on the back with your resumé, include a photo of you wearing contacts. Versatility is splendid. I generally make the little picture black and white because I'm a struggling artist and can't afford color ink for both my headshot *and* resumé. But you can do whatever floats your boat.

Another tip I have is to include your weight. When I first started, I didn't include my weight. I am fit and comfortable with my weight, but I didn't think it seemed necessary. I thought, "Uhhh they're going to see my body in person, they don't need an exact number." However, there are many, MANY times where a director will be looking at your resumé before they see you in person. It's incredibly difficult to judge what someone's body looks like from just a picture of their shoulders and up. If you don't include your weight, a director may think you're heavier than you are and trying to hide it. Or vice versa, if the role requires someone to be a little overweight, your face may make you seem thinner than you are and you won't be considered. So, in my opinion, including your weight helps you. However, if you're not comfortable posting your weight publicly, by all means don't. Do whatever makes you feel most confident without sacrificing auditions.

The middle section is devoted to roles and the bottom section is for training and skills. The top portion, with your stats, should take up about 25%, the middle part should be about 50%, and the bottom portion should be about 25%. You never want your training and skills sections to be larger than your credits section. For one, it seems odd. I mean, if you've got all this training, why aren't you being cast? Secondly, CDs want to see that you're working a lot. *But Meghan, I'm just starting off, I don't have any credits!* Oh child, I hear you. It's tough. But that's why I suggest at first doing anything and everything you can in order to fill up the middle section of your resumé. Eventually you'll be swapping out those student film credits for more prestigious credits. But, until you have Brad Pitt status, you've got to start somewhere.

For film and television credits, do not list the name of the character that you played. Instead put lead, supporting, featured, guest star, or co-star (5 lines or under) under the role column. For theater credits you can list the character name as long as it's a recognizable show. For example, if you portrayed Oedipus in an Off-Broadway production of *Oedipus Rex*, you should definitely put "Oedipus." But if you were the main character in a play your roommate just wrote, simply put "Lead."

If you have done any commercials, you should have a commercial section on your resumé as well. Most agents advise putting "Conflicts Upon Request." Certain companies have actors sign contracts that prevent them from doing advertisements with competing companies, which is known as a conflict of interest. This is also a way to keep your resumé as concise as possible.

Under your special skills section, make sure you only list things you are 100% proficient at. If you're working on a German accent, but haven't mastered it yet, don't put it on your resumé. You need to be able to demonstrate your skills at the drop of hat because you never know what a CD is going to ask you to do.

Keep your resumé clean, precise, and easy to read. Although you may love the CURLZ MT font, it does not have a place on your resumé. You want it to look professional. At first, I thought that I needed to make my resumé unique to stand out from the rest. Instead of aligning all my credits to the left (like you're supposed to), I chose to center them. I thought it looked fun and different, but I immediately got feedback that it looked unprofessional and that I must have been very new. Again, you've got to trick people into thinking you've been acting since you came out of the womb! So again, the simpler, the better.

Now here's the part where I tell you why I don't think resumés matter that much once you're actually in the casting room. Out of all the auditions I've ever been on, I'd say only ten percent of the CDs actually talked to me about my credits. Only TEN percent. That teaches me two things:

1. You should be able to effortlessly talk about any part of your resumé at any given time and hope you sound charming while doing it.

2. CASTING DIRECTORS DON'T REALLY CARE.

In this industry, it really is all about who knows you. I've been cast in some pretty great roles without the director ever looking at my resumé. The CDs care if you have huge blockbuster films or if you have no experience, but they're not super interested in the in-between. When I made my first ever resumé, I decided to include something funny at the bottom. Under Special Skills, my last skill is "Makes a Mean Buffalo Chicken

Wing Dip." I thought it was funny, charismatic, and would start a conversation in the audition room. I've had it on my resumé for years, and it still is to this day. Not a single person has EVER talked to me about it. EVER. That means it's either not that funny (who am I kidding, of course it's funny), or a CD has never actually read my entire resumé. During an audition, they don't really have time anyway, and you want them to be watching your performance. So, make sure your resumé is up-to-date and looks great enough to get you into the room, but do not stress endlessly about it. Put that energy into another facet of your career.

My final note on resumés is to explain how to actually get auditions that get you the roles that make it onto your resumé. I had heard about a casting website called Backstage prior to graduating, but that was the extent of my casting website knowledge. Essentially the only way you will get auditions, and subsequently roles, without an agent is to submit for projects on casting websites yourself. There are numerous casting websites on which you will need to have a profile. The four main ones you'll need to be active on daily are:

corp.castingnetworks.com/la/
www.actorsaccess.com
www.backstage.com
www.castingfrontier.com

These four sites all require a paid membership. You can pay monthly or annually, although I recommend paying annually (see Chapter Seven for more details). Each site requires you to create a profile that includes your headshot and resumé. You can pay extra to include more than one headshot and a reel, something in which you should absolutely invest. Often times, submissions that a have a reel attached to them appear higher in the CD's newsfeed than submissions without attached media. Additionally, there have been several times I've been cast from L.A. Casting Networks without even auditioning. The people who cast me said it was my strong reel that got me the role. Having more than one headshot on these sites is vital, too. You won't want to submit your sexy, cleavage showing headshot for a role where you'll be playing a nun.

Once you've created a profile and paid for a subscription, you're able to submit for whatever roles you want on the website. Besides word of mouth, these are essentially the only ways to submit for roles. When I first moved to Los Angeles, I remember being absolutely clueless about how to get parts in film and television. Thank God a friend of mine had temporarily lived in Hollywood and told me about casting websites, because I honestly wouldn't have known how to even get into an audition room. And now I can be that friend to you! Hooray!

L.A. Casting Networks is most helpful for the California industry, Backstage is most helpful for the New York industry, and Actors Access is awesome for both. Casting Frontier is also good for both coasts, but it's not necessarily one of the heavyweights.

You really have to discipline yourself when it comes to submitting on these sites. The idea is to get as many auditions as possible to statistically increase your chances of actually booking gigs. Therefore, you should aim to submit twice a day, Monday through Friday (there aren't many listings on weekends). I suggest checking the sites at least once in the morning and once in the evening. Checking in the afternoon doesn't hurt either! It shouldn't take more than ten minutes, and you can submit on your phone from anywhere, even on set. And let's be honest: people are lazy. Thus, by submitting constantly, you'll have a huge advantage over your unmotivated peers.

Here we go, the moment you've been waiting for: how to get that sought-after agent. Well guess what? There is no black and white solution. *Gasp!* Are you shocked? Because I was. I mean, in college I kept asking professors how to go about getting representation and they always kind of skirted around the topic. I knew it was going to be difficult, but I had no clue that there weren't specific steps to take. Thus, like most everything I explain in this book, I had to learn through experience.

Now, before I describe what to do to get an agent, I want to explain why it's so important to have one. Firstly, two heads are always better than one. Therefore, two people (you and your agent) working to get you gigs is more productive and efficient than just one. Especially if one of those people is an industry professional whose sole job is to book actors auditions.

Secondly, there's only so much an actor can do on their own, specifically an actor who is new to the industry. Yes, you can self-submit yourself for gigs on L.A. Casting Networks or Actors Access. Yes, you can message friends who are producing their own content. But no, you cannot get yourself into the audition room for a Coen Brothers movie UNLESS you have an agent.

An agent has connections you don't, and they have access to casting breakdowns that you, as an actor without representation, would never be able to see. Also, agents are interested in making money. The only way they make money is if you make money, therefore the jobs they're going to submit you for will be of financial significance. These are all incredibly helpful when it comes to the dream goal of supporting yourself with your acting career. If you want your bills paid by acting, or if you want to have speaking lines in things people will actually have to pay to go see, you need an agent.

Let's get to the nitty gritty of how to get an agent. Again, there is no formula to getting one overnight. Throughout this process, patience will be your best friend. I'm assuming that when you first start looking for an agent, you'll be a non-union member versus a union member. Although the route is similar if you're SAG (Screen Actors Guild), I'll be addressing this topic as if you're non-union.

First and foremost, agents don't want nobodies. Yep, it's the sad truth. They think that if you're brand new to the industry, you won't have the experience or talent required for Casting Directors (CDs) to take you seriously. Which is beyond stupid because how do you get the experience if no one will cast you because you don't have experience?! Have you started screaming into your pillow yet? If so, put the pillow down, take a deep breath, and realize it's do-able. Before you submit for an agency, build your resumé with non-union credits of worth. This means non-union indie films, non-union commercials, and non-union television shows with names that agencies will have heard of. Obviously, indie films won't be recognizable, but if you can land a lead in an indie feature, that at least shows you can handle being a principle in a film.

As far as non-union shows and commercials go, there are tons! Many large companies (Disney, Panera Bread, Samsung—just to name a few) cast non-union actors, who don't have agents, for their advertisements so that they can save money! It makes sense that a struggling company like Disney would cut corners to save money, right? This way, they don't have to pay the actors residuals like they'd have to with union members. There are always posts on casting websites for these major commercials. Typically, the pay is only a couple hundred dollars and they'll never have to pay you again to use your image, BUT you get exposure and a legitimate credit on your resumé! Boom! You're instantly more desirable to an agent.

As far as non-union television credits, there are numerous channels that hire non-union actors as leads. Channels like Investigation Discovery or WEtv hire non-union actors for the cost savings. Plus, these are also posted on casting websites that you can submit to without any representation. Also, everyone and their mother now has their own streaming service and some of these platforms hire non-union actors as well. My advice is to get as many of these official credits on your resumé as possible before submitting to an agent. Student films are an excellent way to get footage and make connections with fellow young artists, but if all you have are student film credits, an agency might not take you seriously. Any credit is better than no credit, but use the student film credits to get you into the casting room of more notable non-union stuff, and then use the non-union legitimate credits to get you an agent.

Similarly, never (almost never) put background work on your resumé. That is one of the first signs of a complete newbie and agencies will avoid you like the plague. Now there have been times where I've put some background credits on my resumé while I was trying to get other work to replace it with. I only included the background work though because I was heavily featured and it was awesome for me to put an ABC sitcom and CollegeHumor credit on my resumé. Plus, I technically had lines, but sneaky ABC decided to play the audio of fifty other voices in addition to my lines so they legally didn't have to credit me or pay me the SAG day player rate and I'm totally not bitter about it at all.

Anywho, building your resumé with meaty non-union parts will help you stand out when submitting to agencies. You'll appear professional and capable. By the way, this is the exact advice I received from a pretty prestigious agency, I'm not just making this stuff up off the top of my head... Or maybe I am, you really don't know, do you?

Now I mentioned training before in a previous chapter, but I'd like to reiterate that an agency will want to see commercial/audition/theatrical workshops and some improv classes as well. (By the way, "theatrical" in the film industry does not mean live stage performances, it means film or television). Again, you'll want a great headshot to catch their attention, but know you'll probably have to get new ones shortly after you sign a contract with them. Plus, as stated before, have an impressive, short reel ready to go.

Once you have your amazing headshot, resumé, and reel, you'll need one final thing in order to land an agent: a referral. This is by far the hardest aspect of getting an agent. For some reason, agencies aren't going to just believe that John Doe is talented because John Doe says so. Instead, they want someone else telling them that John Doe is talented. Super lame, right? Also, this third party cannot be your best friend from grade school, it needs to be a working professional. Even better, a working professional who will actually reach out to the agency on your behalf. It's not as note-worthy if you reach out to an agency and mention someone else's name. If you can get the person to actually reach out to the agency themselves and copy you on the email, you're golden! But the latter is rare, so just being able to use their name will help.

Referrals can be anyone from CDs to actors who are current clients at that agency. Just make sure that when using someone else's name to get your foot in the door, that person actually knows who you are. The worst thing would be if an agency reached out to question your referral about you and your alleged referral says, "[Insert Your Name Here] who?" So, network like crazy among actors and ask if they have an agent and if they are happy with them.

I must warn that I've encountered two different ends of the spectrum when asking actors about their agents:

Reaction #1: MY AGENT SENDS ME OUT ON AUDITIONS TWICE A DAY, I'M SO CONTENT!

Reaction #2: UGH I HATE MY AGENT, THEY LITERALLY NEVER SEND ME OUT!

In my experience, neither of these are 100% truthful. I used to believe everything anyone told me because I was so green to Hollywood. I also grew up in Buffalo,

New York, the "city of good neighbors" where people will literally give you the shirt off their back if you need it. So, I was a little naïve. People would tell me that their representation was sending them out on auditions four times a week. However, their stories didn't make sense because the people claiming they were "auditioning like crazy" were also the people I'd constantly see on set being an extra with me, making minimum wage. Now the contrasting actors, the ones telling me they NEVER got auditions, puzzled me too. At the end of the day, the only way an agent makes money is if their client makes money, so I grew dubious of them too. I quickly learned to take everything with a grain of salt.

Eventually, I learned what questions to ask. If an actor adored their agent because they were getting many auditions, I asked what type of auditions they were being sent out on. Sometimes it was because the person had a special skill like surfing. So yes, they'd audition a lot, but for actual surfer roles, something I wouldn't be able to book because I haven't surfed a day in my life. I'd also ask what communication was like with the agency. Were they easy to get ahold of? Did they return voicemails quickly? etc.

I'd have to do a little bit deeper digging with the people who hated their agencies. I'd first ask when they last got new headshots. If they said three years ago, that was the first red flag. Next, I'd ask if they ever asked their agents for a submission list breakdown. It's basically a list showing what projects they're submitting you for. If the actor admitted they never asked for it despite not getting any auditions, that was another red flag. Finally, if the actor confessed they rarely spoke to their agent, I'd know that it may not be the agency's fault for lack of work, but the client's.

Just because you have an agent does not mean that you stop being proactive. In fact, to this day, I have gone on more auditions that I've gotten for myself than the number of auditions all of my agents/managers combined have gotten me. You must hustle and hustle hard. Therefore, ask questions when people comment on their agencies. Eventually the truth comes out and then you can formulate your own opinion based on facts.

You need to realize that people will lie to you. It's very easy for those in the entertainment industry to exaggerate their accomplishments. People feel foolish saying, "Unfortunately, I haven't had a gig in a few months." Instead, they lie to make themselves feel better. Therefore, you cannot compare yourself to others. Maybe they are working a ton, and maybe they're not. But at the end of the day, their gigs do not affect you. It's not a race, it's not a competition. Allowing yourself to feel down because others are getting more work is a dangerously slippery slope. Focus on yourself. One of my absolute favorite quotes is from comedian Steve Martin. He says, "Be so good they can't ignore you."

Concentrate on your craft and your success. Nothing else matters.

Once you have a kick-butt headshot, resumé, reel, and referral (the referral is not 100% necessary, but so helpful), the next step is figuring out how to contact the agent. On the Screen Actors Guild website, there is a list of all agencies that are SAG affiliated. This is great because all of those agencies are legitimate, follow the rules, and aren't shady. Trust me, there are many sketchy agencies out there. The problem with this list of agencies is that they are the best of the best. People like Jennifer Lawrence and Daniel Radcliffe are signed by these companies. Thus, it'll be much harder to have your email seen. Also, the list doesn't include contact information, so you'll have to Google it.

You can also find agencies in pamphlets sold at bookstores. For example, the Samuel French Bookshop on Sunset Boulevard I mentioned earlier has a frequently updated list of agencies and their addresses/emails. Finally, my favorite way to search for agents and their email addresses is on IMDb Pro. If you pay to get an IMDb account for uploading photos like I mentioned earlier, you'll have access to contact information for basically every agent or manager that's on IMDb! Sometimes agency websites generically state, "submit at this email: submission@talentagency.com." If you email that address, you'll be one of thousands and your message may go to junk mail. But if you email an agent's personal email that you found on IMDb Pro, you're much more likely to reach them. I often look up actors with similar careers as mine on IMDb Pro, see who their agent is, and go about it that way.

When it comes to emailing versus physically mailing a headshot/resumé/cover letter as your submission, I still don't have an exact answer. I've gotten an agent through both methods. However, the last time I got an agent through physically mailing them my goods was in 2014. Everything else since then has been via email. I even scheduled a meeting with a new agency via Instagram once! If you've got extra money and time and want to send out a physical package to an agency, I say why not! However, it seems that nowadays they're more likely to toss that and solely take submissions through emails. The choice, my friend, is yours.

Your email submission should not be a reflection of your amazingly distinctive personality. Yes, you read that correctly, your email should not be overly unique. What I mean is your email should be short, sweet, and to the point. Agents are incredibly busy and if they see an email that is ten pages long, I bet your bottom dollar they will not read it. They also do not have time to read jokes or hear about your difficult childhood. They want to know who you are, where you live, the most recent credit on your resumé, and that's it. I struggled with this at first because I'm a funny, quirky person, and I wanted agents to know that. However, I realized they would discover my eccentricity in our face-to-face meeting. At first, they just needed to be filled in on what I look like, and see that I have a resumé with more on it than the fact that I played Jack in my middle school's production of *Into the Woods Jr.* (Thanks again Mr. Fick for casting me in my first gender-bending role!)

Also, do not put "[Your Name] Headshot" in the subject line of the email. This is the one opportunity you have to stand out a little and ensure they actually open your message. If you have a referral, mention their name. For example, if Will Ferrell is your referral, you better include his name in the subject line. If you're feeling extra bold, simply put "Will Ferrell" in the subject line and the agent might think you're emailing them about one of their top clients. Do this ONLY if Will Ferrell (or whomever you're naming) is actually your referral. If you recently graduated from an impressive acting or improv school, use that. If you just guest starred on a CW show, say "CW Guest Star Seeking New Rep."

Here's an example of what the body of the email should resemble:

Hi Tom Hanks' Acting Agency!
I'm Meghan Deanna Smith, IMTA's Actor of the Year. I just starred in the most recent *Sharknado* film and want to keep this momentum going with some new representation. I'm a big fan of your agency and would love to schedule a meeting ASAP! I've attached my headshot/resumé and below are links to my reels. Looking forward to hearing from you!

It's simple, yet descriptive and should catch their attention long enough to get your foot in the door! Also, I really did star in a Sharknado film called *Sharknado: Heart of Sharkness*, a hysterical mockumentary that just so happens to make the perfect Christmas gift.

If you're seeking an agent and you are already SAG, I recommend the body of your email being different. You can still indicate a recent credit of yours, but you should also include the names of CDs for whom you auditioned and CDs who have booked you. Mentioning CD names in your email will entice agencies/managers because they like to see you have "relationships" with CDs which could lead to more bookings. If you get an in-person meeting with a rep, you should also be prepared to list off the CDs you've auditioned for in the past. Agents hope you already have established connections, making their job easier.

Just for kicks and giggles, I want to share some of my own agent stories so that you're not hearing sugar-coated versions from strangers. I mean technically I am a stranger to you, but I feel like we've connected on a deeper level, and I'm going to trust you with some personal stuff. Also, I'll offer advice on how to interact with your agent by telling you to do the opposite of what I initially did.

The very first agency I signed with was a Commercial Agency in Manhattan. They called me back at an acting competition and I met with them two months later. I remember very vividly saying to the agent when I signed the contract, "You're sure you want me? Oh my goodness, this is the happiest day of my life!" Spoiler Alert: I didn't go on a single audition with that agency, so in hind sight it probably wasn't the happiest day of my life. I was with them for SEVEN months and wasn't sent out on a single audition. Obviously, they were a terrible fit for me. Ideally, I'd be auditioning frequently, or at least more than NEVER, but what I will say is that it was not all their fault. It was my very first agent and I had no clue how to interact with them. I foolishly thought, I'll just do my own thing and they'll do theirs, and eventually we'll both be filthy rich. Wrong.

You and your agent are a team and since you're both working toward the same goal (to get you jobs that pay money), you should be communicating about how to achieve those goals. However, I was clueless. Again, college did not teach us how to talk to agents. While I was with that first agent, I ended up being cast as the lead female in a sketch comedy show at a well-known club in Manhattan (self-booked, of course). It was an amazing step forward in my career. I was so proud, and I didn't even tell them! I don't know why, but talking to my agent seemed daunting and forbidden. Eventually, I left New York City and moved to Los Angeles. I felt discouraged by my representation in New York City, but I didn't realize at first that I was partially to blame! It wasn't until I had made it out west that I realized how poorly I handled things in New York.

You need to talk to your agent… a lot. You need to tell them when you're booking projects on your own to prove your commitment to getting work. If they're paid projects, you also need to tell them because they get 10% of your paycheck. Yes, even if they had nothing to do with booking you the gig, they still get money. It's horrible, but true. You need to tell them when you're taking classes or doing open mic nights. You need to call them and ask, "What else should I be doing?" Never, ever, ever, ever blame them for the lack of auditions. For obvious reasons, they hate that. Instead, always put it on yourself. Consider what you can be doing, whether it's getting new headshots, updating your reel, or simply networking more. You should also occasionally ask your agent if you can stop in to go over pictures or websites, etc. This gives you the opportunity to have face-to-face time. You want your agent to know you and like you. You cannot be just another name on their roster. That is how you fall into the trap of The Land of No Auditions.

When I moved to Hollywood, I mistakenly thought I'd be able to get another agent as quickly as I did in New York City. I was incredibly wrong. The connections I had made from IMTA were essentially all East Coast connections. Thankfully, one CD who had called me back at IMTA was currently residing in Los Angeles. He was kind enough to meet with me and give me some California advice. He told me to use his name as a referral and gave me a list of agencies to reach out to. I physically mailed out cover letters/headshots and emailed everyone on his list. I only received one response and the email stated, "We already have enough blonde clients. Good luck." Sooooo, that didn't go exactly as planned. No one wanted me! I had no choice but to push forward, submit for projects on my own, network like crazy, and a few months later I went through the same exact process of reaching out to agents.

Eventually an agency reached out to me and asked me to come to their open call. I went to the open call, they liked me, and I signed with them the next week. The moral of that story is to persevere! If you're on your A-

Game and keep pushing forward, eventually someone will notice.

I have one more personal agent story to share. At one point in my career, I had an awful agent and a fantastic manager at the same time. My agent was abrasive, discouraging, and any time my phone rang and I saw it was her, my stomach turned into knots. This is certainly not how one should feel, however, I told myself I can deal with a mean agent as long as they're getting me work. The problem was she rarely got me auditions. The agency also sent out an email to all their clients essentially telling us that we needed to come into the office during the lunch hour and bring the agents food to eat while we chatted about our careers. I'm not kidding you, they straight up told us to pay for their food. It was so unprofessional.

Shortly after, I ended up getting cast as a lead in a well-recognized brand commercial. I got the audition myself and I booked the gig myself. I still had to pay my agent 10%, which is fine because I know those are the rules. The commercial pay rate was awesome because they included a separate 10% paycheck specifically for my agent. Unfortunately, my agency took the 10% paycheck and then decided to take an additional 10% out of my personal rate without telling me. This is not allowed, super sketchy, and I was furious. However, after getting that bizarre lunch meeting email and having an extra 10% taken from my paycheck, I was done. I decided

I didn't need that toxicity in my life and I chose to drop them. After all, I had a manager I really loved and I was confident I'd find another agent.

Well, you might have guessed what happened next. Two weeks after I left my terrible agency, out of the blue my manager dropped me. Gave no explanation, just simply said it was time for us to part ways. I was devastated and confused. After all, my IMDb Star Meter was the lowest it had ever been when they dropped me! (IMDb has a Star Meter system you can see once you're a Pro member. It shows where you rank among everyone on the website as far as views go. The lower the number, the more views you get and thus the bigger "star" you are). Being let go by representation made me feel worthless and definitely made me question my ability. At this point, I was completely representation-less.

After a week-long pity party, I started to realize it was my manager's loss, not mine. I only want people representing me who are confident in me and my ability. Plus, I'm extraordinarily talented, stunningly beautiful, and I mean, come on, that management company is totally kicking themselves right now. In conclusion, the moral of that story is a bad agent is better than no agent. You have every right to be dissatisfied with your agency, however, my advice is to seek out new representation before you leave your current one. Once you've been offered representation from a new agency, *then* you can leave your not-so-great one.

So, now that you have all the tools you need to get a good agent, go out there and start submitting! But maybe finish reading this book first, because I'm an incredibly sensitive person and I'll know if you've put me on the back burner. Thanks.

CHAPTER FIVE

SCREEN ACTORS GUILD AND UNION MUMBO JUMBO

When I was in school, I remember briefly learning about unions. And by briefly, I mean I was told they exist. That was pretty much it. All I knew was that it cost money to join, and since I was incredibly broke, I avoided union stuff. However, when I got to Los Angeles and was looking to sign with film/television agencies, I instantly realized I needed to learn more about what exactly the Screen Actors Guild was.

SAG is a union very similar to unions other industries have. It's essentially a guild to protect the rights of the workers and provide you with benefits. It also costs THREE THOUSAND DOLLARS to join. (Or at least it does as of the day I'm writing this. It's possible by the time you read this, it'll have increased. Actually, it's probable it will have increased. My apologies in advance.) Did your heart just stop? Sorry about that, I should have warned you. Yes indeed, it costs thousands of dollars to join which is something I've always felt was so unfair. Before you join the union, you're only getting non-union work which typically pays minimum wage. How in the world can you set aside three grand when you're only making minimum wage? Gah! However, once you join the union, you will be an official SAG member just like Scarlet Johansson and Pee Wee Herman, to name a couple of the greats. That also means you'll be a small fish in a very, very big pond.

Should you join SAG right away? The overwhelming advice I've been given is no, do not join SAG right away. Like I mentioned, if you join right away, you'll be a minnow in the Atlantic, whereas if you stay non-union for a bit, you'll be the big kid on campus. People in SAG are typically trained, working, and professional. People who are non-union are often uneducated and learning. You have the chance to stand out in non-union audition rooms because you'll be more qualified and experienced than the majority of the non-union auditionees. Once you join though, you'll be competing against Bradley Cooper. Do you really want to set yourself up for that kind of failure right away? Plus, if you're union, you legally cannot work non-union jobs, which does limit what gigs you can get for yourself.

An agent also told me that sometimes actors will join SAG too soon and their resumés will stink. They'll join right away because they have the money, but they don't have strong enough credits on their resumé to back up their SAG status. Subsequently, Casting Directors (CDs) get confused as to why you're SAG with none of the experience.

Now there's another aspect to the union. You simply cannot join just because you have $3,000. You must also be SAG Eligible. You can become SAG Eligible in one of two ways:

1. You can do background work as a non-union extra. Each day you do background work, you receive a non-union 'voucher' which is basically your paycheck. Television shows and feature films also hire union extras. If for some reason a union extra does not show up to set on a day you're working, a Production Assistant could decide to give you their union voucher. If you're able to snag three union vouchers (or "Golden Tickets" as we like to call them in the background industry), you are eligible to join SAG!

Does this method sound incredibly luck driven and unfair to you? Well, you're right! It is! In fact, I did background work on and off for almost three years and never received a single union voucher. Not one! However, I did encounter numerous people who received all three union vouchers within a couple weeks of doing background work. It was so imbalanced and frustrating. My advice is to not rely on the background method to becoming SAG, but to each his own. If you're a super lucky person, maybe this route is best for you.

2. You can be part of a SAG New Media production. There is a way to make whatever content you're working on a SAG production, simply by filling out a lot of paperwork. There are so many indie projects and aspiring filmmakers who turn their projects into union productions by following the SAG New Media route. The instructions of how to do it are on the SAG website and pretty much anyone can do it. This is how I became SAG Eligible. I got cast as the lead in a five-minute horror short and the director filled out all the SAG New Media paperwork to get me my union status. A month after we filmed, I got a letter in the mail from the Screen Actors Guild stating I could finally join if I had the money. I was beyond thrilled.

This route is so much easier in my opinion because there are so many New Media projects listed on casting websites. Or, if you're ambitious enough, develop your own project and fill out the paperwork. Relying on yourself will be way more dependable than praying a Production Assistant hands you a Golden Ticket.

I have found that the best position to be in is SAG Eligible, which occurs after you've attained three union vouchers or done a New Media project, but have not yet paid the $3,000 joining fee. SAG Eligible means you can still work non-union gigs, but you can also audition for anything union. If you get the union gig, you simply have to pay the fee and you're in. Agents loved that I was SAG Eligible because they could submit me for double the work: non-union and union jobs. My advice is to start saving three grand as soon as possible. Do as many impressive non-union roles as you can. Become SAG Eligible through a New Media project. Wait to join until you book your first union gig, and then put that first union paycheck toward joining! Easy peasy!

CHAPTER SIX

I hope you become an auditioning pro very early on in your career. Thankfully I went through my awkward, unconfident auditioning stage during my college years, so when I made it out into the real world, I was ready. But it's possible you're not 100% ready yet, so here's some advice to get you there quicker.

Auditioning should be fun. Why? Because you're performing, and isn't that what you want to do for the rest of your life? An incredibly intelligent, fabulous professor of mine, Amanda Lytle-Sharpe, once taught me to treat auditions like mini performances. Why the heck shouldn't you? You get to do something you're passionate about in front of an audience. Albeit that audience may just be a Casting Director (CD) and a camcorder, but still!

Another thing to remember when auditioning is to not try so hard. A CD can sense when someone's forcing something and immediately gets turned off. They can smell desperation too, which is another no-no. The CD wants to think you're just naturally talented. Now, that doesn't mean you shouldn't put a lot of effort and time into prepping for your audition, but when you're in the actual audition room, you need to make it seem like acting is effortless for you.

One time I auditioned for a commercial for a tablet with voice command. When I arrived to the audition location, the CD instructed the auditionees that once we got into the room, we'd hold a tablet and pretend like we were using voice command to save some things on an electronic to-do list. The examples he gave of what to say were: "Call Mom" or "Wash Car." Super simple. He then said, "Do NOT show off. I had some girl earlier today sing her to-do list just to prove that she had a good voice. There is no singing and she will not be cast."

Although I found this incredibly funny and immediately pictured a stereotypical theater girl singing her to-do list to the melody of *Annie*'s "Tomorrow," it was a great example of what not to do. Just because you have an amazing Scottish accent does not mean you should find a way to incorporate it into a dramatic monologue, just like that girl should not have sang just because she can. These things come across as pushy and desperate.

Conversely, you do need to stand out and be bold. Finding a balance between being daring, but not aggressive, is extraordinarily difficult.

Another time, I auditioned for a Samsung Android commercial where I needed to write a note on my phone using a stylus. It was supposed to be something simple, but random, similar to the tablet commercial audition. I thought I'd be witty and audacious, so I wrote "Apple sucks." Really, really funny, right? Well, the CD didn't think so. He got mad, said it was inappropriate, explained that wasn't what they were looking for, and believe it or not I didn't get the part. That was a great example of how I tried too hard. Don't do that.

Also, side note: when auditioning for commercials for products, they will take a close-up photo or video of your hands. Make sure your nails are dirt free and trimmed before all auditions! You can wear nail polish, but it shouldn't be a very bold/neon color nor should it be chipped. Also, moisturize your hands before the audition. That means you too, men! A CD doesn't want to cast a pair of dry, crusty hands to demonstrate their product on national television.

Now that we've entered the age of technology, you may not always hand in a physical copy of your headshot and resumé. Since essentially all submissions are done online, they'll already have an electronic copy and may not need a physical one. However, always, always, always bring a headshot and resumé with you just in case. If you don't have one with you and they ask for one, you will seem incredibly unprofessional. Plus, when they're sifting through the copies of auditionees' materials, your picture won't be there, and they'll most likely forget about you. My best advice is to always keep at least one headshot/resumé in your car! (If you live in New York City and don't have a car, because, like, who drives a car in Manhattan? I suggest you keep an extra headshot/resumé in your public transportation bag.) You never know when you're going to get a last-minute audition, so it's better to be safe than sorry.

Another random piece of audition advice I received during an acting workshop is to wear the color blue. Why? I actually don't know. The director giving the workshop said for some reason the majority of actors he cast wore blue to the audition. Was he talking out of his pooper? Probably. But he had directed Julia Roberts once, and blue looks good on me, so why not?

In college, whenever I auditioned for shows, I had to prepare a one to two minute monologue and dress nicely. The only time we read sides from the actual production was in the callback. This is NOT how the real world works. In the dozens upon dozens of film and stage auditions I've attended, only TWICE did I have to prepare a monologue. That's because in the real world, you're auditioning for one project, not an entire school's season of shows. Therefore, the "outside of college world" wants to hear you speak the actual lines of the character for whom you are auditioning. They also want to see you dressed as the character, not just "looking nice." If you're auditioning to be a nurse, wear scrubs. If you're auditioning to be a country boy who rides horses, wear cowboy boots. You should be the character in as many physical ways as possible.

I often receive a script ahead of time; but there are numerous times where I've been given the script as soon as I walked into the audition room. There were also times I prepared the script they sent me, performed it, and then the director decided she wanted to see me read a different excerpt from the script. I was handed an unfamiliar piece of material to perform on the spot. What all of this means is BECOME A PRO AT COLD READING. Maybe you have the acting chops of Leonardo DiCaprio, but when given a random script out of the blue, you stumble over words, get shaky hands, and forget every acting technique you've ever learned. Do not fret. Cold reading is a skill that can be learned. The key is practice. Try acting out loud as many random passages as you can to exercise your cold reading muscles. If you can make the back of your cereal box sound eloquent and entertaining, you're going to be a movie star. This skill will absolutely help you stand out during the auditioning process.

SELF-TAPES

More and more recently, "self-tape auditions" have become popular. Instead of showing up to a casting location, the production asks you to film your audition yourself and electronically send it to them. There are pros and cons to this. A con is that you can't guarantee they'll actually watch your tape. Even if they do, they may not watch the whole thing. However, a pro is that you can choose your best take to send! If you mess up the first time, just film it again.

However, there is an art to self-submissions. You need to have good lighting, good sound, and a buddy to operate the camera/read opposite of you. Thankfully smart phones have excellent cameras today, so that helps with the quality. Trying to find a well-lit spot in your home can be tricky, so just be prepared to move a lot of lamps. Keep in mind there cannot be any harsh shadows behind you or on your face (daylight is the best). Also, your background should be plain. You may adore the giant watercolor elephant canvas hanging on your wall that your best friend got you, but it should not make it on camera for a self-submission. Do not include anything to distract the viewer from you.

Now, does all of that sound painstakingly difficult? Well, honestly, it *is* incredibly difficult. Thankfully, I have found some amazing ways to make self-tapes both easier and more professional looking. For example, I purchased a pop-out, muslin backdrop online for about fifty-five dollars. It's essentially a five-foot by six-foot background that folds into a tiny circle when you're not using it and it has saved my life. I used to spend hours trying to find a section of my apartment with a plain background. But now that I have the backdrop, I can literally do my audition anywhere! This means I can film right next to my huge window providing the most killer natural light. Before I purchased the backdrop, there was no space where I could take advantage of natural light.

Another big advantage of the pop-out is that it gives the illusion you've filmed your audition at a studio because the solid colored background looks so professional. You will also need to invest in a tripod. It can be impossible to position the camera at the exact angle while leaning the phone against a shaky nightstand table and a stack of books. The tripod will come in handy. Or, you can just live with someone who has an amazing tripod already and lets you use it at all times of the night. (BRITTANY, YOU'RE AN ANGEL AND I'M FOREVER INDEBTED TO YOU).

The trickiest part for me about self-tapes is the reader. You absolutely need someone else's voice off camera. You simply can't do both voices in a scene. Trust me, I've tried. One time I literally recorded my own voice reading the other parts and left space for me to respond to them in real time. To put it kindly, it was a disaster. So, you need a buddy. I thought it'd be easy since at one point, I had three other roommates. Alas, their schedules never seemed to coordinate with mine. I've been forced to film auditions at very random hours of the night with roommates, friends, lovers, and acquaintances. Find an audition partner. It'll come in handy when you get a last-minute self-submission that needs to be sent in by midnight. Also, send in your tape as soon as possible. If you get a self-submission that needs to be sent in within three days, send it on day one. Often times the CDs will watch the auditions as they come in. If they find someone they like before day three, they'll just cast that person and not even watch your tape. Sending your audition in sooner can only help you.

If you're in a terrible pickle and truly cannot find anyone to read the other character's lines, I recommend the "Phone Technique" as an absolute last resort. This entails emailing someone your script, calling them on speakerphone, placing the phone near the camera, and having them do the scene with you as if they were actually in the room. It's not ideal, but if it's your only option, it might help you out in a pinch.

Finally, I want to provide some audition acting advice. I know I said this book wouldn't teach you how to act, however, I feel this discovery is important. When I was in college, one of my classmates told me I was her favorite scene partner to act with. It was one of the greatest compliments I've received and it had a profound impact on my acting from that point forward. She never explained specifically why she felt that way, so I went on a mission to figure out what about myself as an actress made her say that. Eventually, it clicked. Above everything in this world, I adore listening. Truly hearing people and their stories brings me such great joy. Not everyone enjoys listening. In fact, I know many people who solely like to talk about themselves. I realized there are actors out there who also don't enjoy listening. As an actor, that's what I bring to my scene partners that not everyone else does: I listen. As a character, as a person, as a friend, I listen.

There's a beautiful quote I really connect with about listening. It says, "The biggest issue with communication is that we do not listen to understand, we listen to reply." If you can learn to apply this to your auditions, your projects, and your characters, you will experience so much more success. Do not simply wait for your cue line. Instead, truly listen to what's being given to you, and respond naturally. It will do wonders.

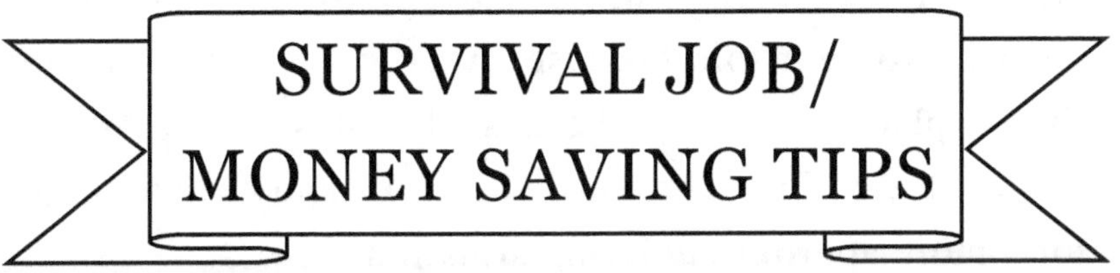

CHAPTER SEVEN

SURVIVAL JOB

When you finally move out to the major industry hub closest to you, you're going to need a "survival job." Although I hope you start getting paid acting gigs right away, realistically that's going to take time. In fact, you'll need to do a lot of unpaid projects at first (indie shorts, student films, etc.) in order to build resumé credits, get reel footage, and network with people. Therefore, you're going to need income to pay bills, especially since New York City and Los Angeles are pretty much the most expensive cities in America. How fun! The best advice I can give is to make the move when you have a large savings. Looking for decent roommates and waiting to hear back about job interviews can take time. Plus, all the while you'll continue to be paying for acting 'stuff' which can be financially draining. Therefore, having a good financial cushion will be a godsend. That money cushion will also help prevent you from settling for an unsafe situation simply because you feel like you have to get a place right away. I almost moved into a crappy house with eight men in their forties when I was only twenty-two years old because I was feeling desperate to find a place. However, because I had set aside some money, I was able to be a little bit picky and keep looking for a more appropriate living situation.

My next best advice is to do background work (BG). Through BG, you can get paid to be an extra in films and television shows. Two places you should register with in order to start being an extra are Central Casting and Rich King Casting. As a struggling artist moving to a new city, it's amazing for several reasons:

Reason #1: You're earning an income. You only make minimum wage, but you earn overtime if you're on set for more than eight hours and let's be honest—film sets are incredibly inefficient.

Reason #2: You get to be on legit, major budget sets. I've been an extra in a wide variety of productions, everything from Mark Walhberg feature films to Amy Poehler sitcoms to Liev Shriber dramas. You get to experience firsthand how major sets function, and you can learn so much through observation. For example, I remember having no clue what a "stand-in" was (a person who's paid to do the main actor's blocking while the crew get lighting and camera angles correct) or what a "PA" was (a Production Assistant is a person who runs around putting out fires on set). You learn the lingo and you learn how to behave on set. Doing BG is an incredibly valuable experience.

Reason #3: It's a one-day commitment. Typically, you're booked as an extra for one day at a time which is awesome because that allows you to pick and choose your schedule. If you've got an audition on Tuesday, but no work Wednesday, you can seek background work only for Wednesday. I found BG so helpful and compatible for my schedule. Other jobs have set schedules and don't allow you to miss your shift, even if you have the audition of a lifetime. However, with BG, you choose your schedule. If you've been cast in an indie short that's shooting over the weekend, you don't need to call people to cover your shift. Instead, you just don't book yourself for extra work that weekend. For that reason alone, it was an awesome survival job.

Reason #4: It's a perfect way to network. Not only are you on set with professional industry peeps who've got their stuff together, you're also on set with dozens of other struggling artists. I made so many friends and connections through doing BG. In fact, some of my IMDb credits came from other extras casting me in their projects. I always make it a goal to befriend at least one actor every time I'm on set.

Besides BG, I recommend searching for jobs with flexible schedules. One of my absolute best friends in New York City is a personal assistant to a B-List celebrity. He loves it because he's able to audition/attend rehearsals in between doing tasks for his semi-celebrity boss. One of my actor friends in Los Angeles does all the social media for a company, so he's able to do their Twitter/Facebook updates and messaging while he's out and about.

I briefly mentioned the role of a stand-in, which is another cool way to get paid to work in the industry. There are several casting companies that hire actors to be stand-ins and essentially all you have to do to get booked is create a profile online. (My favorite company for this is Onset Productions—Murray, you're the man!) I've stood in for Indie films, projects on MTV, and even Food Network shows. Basically, any program you watch on television, be it fictional, reality, or competition, needs stand-ins. For the most part, the job is pretty easy. You just stand.

I also was lucky enough to find a fabulous family online that needed a nanny one day a week. For years I babysat for this local family every Thursday. What was excellent about it was that I knew every Thursday I was guaranteed to get cash. It was the only constant in my life and it was amazing. Acting gigs, even background work, can be unpredictable, yet I knew I had at least one paycheck a week. Plus, I got really good at cleaning up poop and heating up hot dogs, soooo there's that.

There are many options out there for you to find a flexible job that pays money, yet fits your acting lifestyle. I know a lot of actors are the stereotypical waiters. I've been there, done that, but I HATED it. It's stressful, not always worth it financially, and I found it so difficult to get people to cover shifts last minute if I got an audition or was cast in a project. My opinion is to avoid serving if you can, however, to each his own. If bringing customers chips and salsa at Chili's and then getting a fourth of the tip you deserve brings you happiness, then by all means—serve away.

The one major issue with having a survival job is learning when to say "no." What I mean is that there will always be several opportunities that conflict with one another. For example, you may get an audition for 2 p.m., but you're scheduled to make drinks at Starbucks at 2 p.m. If you go to the audition, you'll make your agent happy, and you have a possibility of getting cast which will make you some money whenever that project shoots. However, getting cast is not guaranteed. Furthermore, attending the audition doesn't pay your electric bill like you know your Starbucks shift will. At the same time, many agencies will drop you if you don't attend an audition, and Starbucks could fire you for not coming to work when scheduled. The dilemma is awful and the struggle is real.

At the end of the day, you didn't move to Los Angeles or New York or Chicago to become a professional barista, you came to be a successful actor. I've let that mentality guide my decision making, but I've also turned down some potential acting opportunities in order to pay my bills with my survival job. There is no solution, but just know that every single actor has this problem. Trying to find balance is key.

MONEY SAVING TIPS

You're going to want to find as many ways to save money as you can in order to afford better quality classes, headshots, business cards, etc.

All of the casting websites (L.A. Casting Networks, Backstage, Actors Access, Casting Frontier) offer monthly payments, or you can pay a larger sum for a six month or year subscription. When you pay for more months at a time, they always offer a discount so I definitely suggest doing this. Also, once you join SAG, they offer numerous discounts including a significant discount on your IMDb account!

For several years, I also saved a buttload of money by finding a creative living situation. I moved into a two-bedroom apartment with two other girls. The other two girls took the bedrooms and I took half of the living room. I was able to section it off with furniture and black-out curtains, and no one ever had to walk through my room to get to any other section of the apartment. Plus, the way we arranged things, we still had a living room with a couch and television. It helped tremendously that my roommates were super courteous and considerate, and it was amazing because THREE of us were responsible for rent for a TWO-bedroom place. We all saved so much money and I loved the fact that my rent wasn't outrageous. So, keep an open mind when it comes to your living arrangement as creativity can go a long way. However, it's important to also consider your safety and comfort when exploring cost-effective options.

My final, kind of bizarre, way to earn money in Los Angeles or New York is to compete on a game show. Game shows are often looking to cast people who are comfortable in front of a camera (i.e., actors). Now, you're not "hired as an actor" because you're not acting. Instead, you're playing a game that just so happens to be filmed. But the game show Casting Directors (CDs) like to know the people competing can hit their mark, act natural in front of an audience, and not drop an F-bomb on national television. I've had some success competing on game shows that have definitely helped alleviate the financial burdens of Hollywood. Plus, I got to hug Wayne Brady on "Let's Make a Deal," so there's really nothing I'm prouder of.

What's also interesting about game shows is that before a new show gets picked up by a station, it needs to be played in front of the network so the network can decide if the show will be successful or not. These presentations are called "game show run-throughs." Every game show you've ever watched was first presented to a network as a "game show run-through." They get the host, network executives, and contestants together in a small room and play the game. The contestants are usually hired actors who get paid for doing the run-through. They hire actors because again, they'll be professional, high energy, and won't utter curse words in front of the CEO of NBC. I've been hired numerous times on casting websites to do game show run-throughs and I love it! It's awesome to get paid to play games and it's usually no longer than a four-hour day. Plus, I'm pretty much a champion at board games and one of the most competitive people on Earth, so it's a great outlet for me to crush people. No really, I dare you to beat me at Taboo.

There are many great ways to save money and earn some extra cash when trying to make it in the acting industry. To conclude, spending a couple years in a living room will be totally worth it when you're eventually rich and famous, living on your private yacht.

CHAPTER EIGHT

Here we are folks, in the Golden Age of Social Media. It kind of makes me cringe writing that. It's bizarre to think that we live in a world where it's normal for toddlers to operate iPads and cars to drive themselves. But we must adapt to the times, especially when it comes to our career. Before moving out to the City of Angels, I had no idea how imperative social media would be. That's why I want to warn you now of its importance so you can start building your own Twitter empire ASAP.

We all have that one friend who posts twelve times a day using a million hashtags and so obviously wants attention. Well, you need to become that person. You need to embrace social media in every way. That includes Facebook, Instagram, Twitter, YouTube, Snapchat, TikTok, etc. Why? For one, you need to advertise yourself. You are a "product" after all. More importantly, Casting Directors (CDs) want to see that you have fans. They want to know that people are following you and invested in what you do. The reason behind this is because CDs have begun to look at actors as free advertising. They will cast an actor who's not that talented, but has a million followers, over an actor who's incredibly talented, but has only 100 followers. They know when the million-follower actor posts about it, the project will be advertised to a million people, which will help make them more money.

Personally, I hate it. There have been numerous auditions I haven't been able to attend simply because I didn't have at least 10,000 followers. Be prepared. Furthermore, there are now talent agencies that have specific agents for "Digital Influencers." That's what the industry is slowly transforming into.

Another aspect of the social media craze you need to partake in is posting your own videos, be it on YouTube, TikTok, Vimeo, etc. This is crucial for a few different reasons. For one, the more exposure you have, the better. This way when someone in the industry Googles you, they'll be directed to not only your Facebook page, but also a video account with videos of you actually performing. It's one thing to see a pretty face, but it's another thing to see that pretty face acting, even if it is a silly short film on YouTube. Thus, you should have content up on the interwebs for all to see.

Now, there will be many projects that you'll have participated in that aren't viewable online. Sometimes it legally can't be seen online if it's in a festival, sometimes directors can be picky about who views their content for free, or sometimes, and this is my favorite example, the project never gets finished. Whatever the case may be, you can't use these as excuses for why you don't have videos of you performing online. Obviously, you'll have your reel posted, but there needs to be more than just a two-minute video showcasing you. You need to have an online presence as an actor and as an artist. I suggest writing, filming, acting in, and editing your own content. Create a YouTube channel or start a website and make stuff that you're proud of that demonstrates who you are as a performer.

Some of you are probably thinking, *But Meghan! I'm an actor, not a writer!* My response to that is: suck it up and write! Learning to write a script, even if it's one page long, will help you become a better actor. Also, filming/directing your content will help you become more experienced in the film industry in general. I'm not asking you to change your career path from a person in front of the camera to a person behind the camera. What I am saying is that it is not that hard to write a few lines, press a record button, deliver a great performance, and upload it to the world-wide web. You don't have to make a piece worthy of the Sundance Film Festival, just something small you're proud of (but something that's lit well, don't forget proper lighting!).

When I first got to Los Angeles, I had known that YouTube videos were becoming more and more socially relevant, but I was reluctant to start my own channel. It seemed hard and intimidating and, to be honest, I felt a little too lazy to venture down the path of conceptualizing my own content. Then I had two pretty big wake up calls.

Wake Up Call #1: I was cast as a "Teenage Girl Screaming Fan" background actor for a feature film that was going to be on Netflix. I know what you're thinking, and no, it wasn't my big break. Weird, right? Anyway, I arrive on set and am told the lead actor of the film is some young male Vine star (you know, back when Vine, MySpace, and walking your pet dinosaur was a thing). I wasn't super familiar with the elite Viners, so it wasn't as big of a deal to me as it was to some of the other young, star-struck extras. In fact, it upset me a little to know some kid who can only hold people's attention with a six-second selfie video was going to be the principle actor in a feature film, something I'd been working my butt off to achieve. But, you must remember, jealousy in Hollywood can bring you down a horrid path. The moment you compare yourself to someone else, you're doomed. I held my head up high and decided to be the best screaming fangirl there was.

The scene was simple. The main actor walked among a crowd of screaming fans and he had to smile at them all, wave, and then walk onto a bus. We did it several times and then the crew decided it was time for a close-up. Since the background actors weren't going to be seen in such a tight shot, they had us extras take a break and step off set for a second. They then did the same exact scene, but this time the actor didn't smile at fans or wave. He stone facedly walked onto the bus. The director yelled cut and asked the kid what was wrong and why he didn't wave at the fans this time. The actor replied, "Well they're not here anymore, right? Why would I wave to no one?" The director had to take TEN WHOLE MINUTES to explain to this young man that when they do close-up shots, even though his face is the only one seen on screen, technically those fans are still there screaming and still need to be acknowledged.

Now I by no means feel like that actor was stupid. Instead, I grew upset at the CD for casting someone who is NOT an actual actor and who has never set foot on a professional set before. This kid knows how to hold his cell phone in front of his face and give a charming smirk. He does not know how to hit his mark, remember complicated blocking, try to achieve his objective, and stay in his light all at the same time. He was never trained on how to do any of that. Regardless, he still got cast as lead in a feature film solely because he had over 5 million followers on Vine and the producers knew his fans would see the movie. It was a crappy realization, but also empowering, because I was slowly but surely learning ways to "make it" in Hollywood.

Wake Up Call #2: I worked on a film with a B-List celebrity who immediately clicked with me. He loved my acting style, enjoyed my comedy, and wanted to collaborate on a project. We came up with an awesome idea that was going to boost his career and finally put me on the scene. This was what was going to pave the way for my success as an actress and I was elated. I agreed to do a lot of the planning and pre-production work because he was busy with some other B-List films. I put HOURS upon HOURS of work into planning this project/film. It consumed my life. I couldn't sleep at night because my mind was always racing with ideas and fantasizing about what my career was going to be like after this film premiered.

Then, three months into our project, he quit. Out of nowhere, he essentially said, "I'm sorry, I'm out. This has been great, but it's not going to work out anymore, I'm going to focus on other stuff. Good luck in the future." And that was it. I was devastated. Absolutely crushed. But it wasn't until I got "dumped" by my first real Hollywood gig that I had an epiphany. I realized if I was capable of putting that much work into a project like that, one that wasn't guaranteed, why couldn't I put all that effort into my own content? So, I talked to my two favorite people in Los Angeles and starting brainstorming. I told Brittany Meyerhardt, my talented roommate-at-the-time/director, and Curtis Kingsley, an insanely funny comedian/actor/writer, that I wanted to collaborate on a YouTube channel. I wanted us to create our own comedy sketches and upload them online. At a minimum, we'd be perfecting our craft and doing something we love. In the best-case scenario, we could garner lots of exposure, get cast in features like that Vine star, and actually make a name for ourselves doing something we're passionate about. That was how "We Find Us Funny," my YouTube channel, started.

Curtis, Brittany, and I are still making sketches and posting them to our "We Find Us Funny" YouTube channel, and it's one of the best things that could have happened to me. I'm able to exercise my acting skills, write and develop ideas that actually showcase my specific talents, and have fun with my two favorite humans at the same time. It helped me keep my acting muscles strong even when jobs were scarce, and it gave me a plethora of awesome videos to share with CDs, directors, or anyone of worth in the industry. Brittany often talks about how she wants "We Find Us Funny" to become an actual production company in the future, and knowing that we have paved a way for ourselves by making silly online videos is really fulfilling.

Long story short: Create. Post. Generate. Embrace social media. If you've always felt you'd make a perfect Elphaba from *Wicked* in a black and white film noir, MAKE IT. You never know what may come of it and the chance to succeed far outweighs the risk of failing.

CONCLUSION

Well here we are: the completion of the book. At this point, you've probably realized that I am a true genius. And for that, you're welcome. But in all seriousness, writing the conclusion has been the most challenging aspect of the book for me because I don't want it to be over! But all good things must come to an end and I need to thank you, my magnificent reader. You're the reason this book came to be and I'm supremely grateful.

I know I've shared a lot of different strategies and techniques with you, but I think the most important thing to take away from this guide is confidence. Believing in yourself and loving yourself while trudging through the performance industry is imperative. Artists are quick to get depressed because this career path can set you up for a lot of failure. However, you need to use the failures as motivation to work harder.

So, here's some final thoughts: be prepared to physically run a lot from audition to audition, get comfortable changing outfits in your car frequently, and stop wasting time binge watching TV shows while claiming it's "research" for your craft. Work hard and remember to always derive joy from acting. There are people across the country who would kill to go on auditions and work on sets, but they'll never have the courage to pursue their dreams. Anytime you're depressed that you're only a movie extra for example, keep in mind some mailman in Minnesota would probably think you're the coolest person ever.

It's also important to remember that you might not become a household name. A successful actor does not always equate to a famous actor. Realistically, your goal should be to live off of acting. If exposure and fame come from it, so be it. But this book is not intended to make you the next Emma Stone, it's intended to help you pay your bills with acting gigs, something that can be super gratifying. If you do happen to become the next Emma Stone though, I will take 100% of the credit.

For now, I bid you adieu. I love you and you're perfect. Now go kick some acting butt.

ABOUT THE AUTHOR

Meghan Deanna Smith is a trained actress, comedian, and writer, currently living in Los Angeles, California. She began acting at a young age, and continued on to receive a Bachelor of Fine Arts Degree in Theater Performance from Niagara University.

Smith has taken dozens of acting, voice over, stage combat, singing, commercial acting, dance, screen writing, modeling, and audition classes/seminars and uses that knowledge daily while she auditions and books work as an actress. She is happily married and the proud fur-mom of a rescue dog.

Instagram & Twitter: @megdeannasmith
Facebook: www.facebook.com/megdeannasmith
IMDb: www.imdb.me/meghandeannasmith

www.ingramcontent.com/pod-product-compliance
Lightning Source LLC
Chambersburg PA
CBHW061749050726
47598CB00002B/655